The Ultimate Life Plan

How To Create, Design And Manifest Your Ideal Life

Introduction

I want to thank you for purchasing this Kindle book titled, "The Ultimate Life Plan - How To Create, Design And Manifest Your Ideal Life".

This book will reveal just that - how you can learn from some of the most successful people in the world and apply their lessons to creating and manifesting your ultimate dream life.

It all starts with a vision and a purpose, which this book will show you exactly how to do. As the Bible says, "Without a vision, people perish"... and it's so true. Everyone needs a compelling future and something to look forward to. Unfortunately, most people don't know what they want and therefor will never get anywhere.

This book goes beyond just creating a vision, but goes into specific goals and action plans for you to create to ultimately turn your dreams into a reality. This book can also be considered a powerful TIME and LIFE MANAGEMENT SYSTEM.

If you apply these principles to your life, and actually take the time to answer these questions, you will possess a powerful system for you to follow on a weekly and daily basis, as well as design the ideal life of your dreams.

If you received some value from this Kindle book, I'd love for you to leave a review on Amazon.com where you purchased the book.

Thank you and enjoy!

Life Management System

Do you want to find out how you can manage your life so that you can be more productive, balance, and create lasting fulfillment?

Most people struggle with balance in their lives and are often stressed when trying to manage all the different areas of life - whether it be your career, business, finances, relationships, health, fitness, family, friends, etc... that's why it's imperative to have a system that you can follow so that you can really manage all the areas of your life effectively and make continual progress towards where you want to be.

This book will help address this challenge. I have a specific system that I've modeled from Tony Robbins in his Time Of Your Life program - it's called his **RPM Life Management System (RPM stands for Rapid Planning Method)**. It's really revolutionized my life in many ways, and I've since modified it and created a spreadsheet that works well with the method.

In this book, I'm going to go into details about the entire process - it will show you exactly how to create an ultimate vision, purpose, identity, 1-year/90-day/30-day outcomes, action plans, and how to measure yourself on a weekly basis. Not only that, but you will go through this process and create a vision/purpose/identity for each area of your life, which will create even more clarity to what you want in your life and help you achieve it faster.

Your Ultimate Vision For Your Life

The first step in designing your life is to create a compelling vision of who you'll become and what you want your life to ultimately be like. This is a very powerful part of the process, as your ultimate vision is what will drive you and really excite you - **it gives you something to look forward to on a continual basis.**

Without a vision, people perish.

I've found that what most people lack in life is a really compelling vision. In fact, it's not that most people are lazy or bored, it's that they have an impotent vision - nothing to look forward to. Without anything to look forward to, what reason do you have to do anything? What reason do you have to get out of bed?

In the video, you can see that I've used powerful language and really described who I want to be and what I want my life to be about. The key is to discover the right vision for you, as it's different for everyone. **What would really excite you? What do you want your life to be about? If there were no limits or obstacles, what would you want your ultimate vision to be?** These are all great questions to ask yourself.

Take a moment and answer these questions. You can write it out in a journal, or you can use the spreadsheet that you can keep on your computer, or keep it online using Google documents. I personally keep it online on Google documents so that I can access it anywhere in the world (including on my iPhone in the video), and I'm continually updating it.

- **What is the ultimate vision for my life?**
- **What do I want my life to be about?**
- **If there were no limits, what would be possible for my life?**
- **What do I want for each area of my life?**

Examples:

"To be a successful leader, coach, speaker, blogger, and internet marketer that creates incredible products and services that makes a difference in the lives of others worldwide."

"To build my own foundation to help those in need."

"To be 180 lbs at 8% body fat."

Your Ultimate Purpose For Your Life

Your ultimate purpose for your life is what will give you the fuel to really go after your ultimate vision. It's the REASONS to get yourself to follow through - the fuel for the life. **It all starts with asking yourself, "Why do I want this?".** For me personally, I just make a list of reasons of why I want to achieve this vision - why I'll do whatever it takes. You want to really think about it, as when you want something bad enough, you will do almost ANYTHING to make it happen. When you discover your powerful purpose and reasons why, you'll create ultimate leverage on yourself.

If you have a strong enough WHY, you can make anything happen.

Ask yourself these questions and get out your journal or spreadsheet to fill it in:

- **Why do I want to fulfill this ultimate vision for my life?**
- **What will achieving this ultimate vision give me?**
- **How will achieving this ultimate vision enhance each area of my life?**
- **What will it cost me if I don't make it happen? What are the ultimate consequences?**
- **What are my reasons for following through?**

- **How will I be able to help more people?**

Examples:

"To be a role model and inspiration to others."

"To be financially free - to do what I want, when I want."

"To be happy and really live life to the fullest - to do what I was put here for."

Your Identity

Your identity is essentially who you are and what your stand for in your life. It's all about how you define yourself, as your identity is merely a sum total of your beliefs.

Human beings will do anything to remain consistent with how we define ourselves.

When you really discover who you are and begin living by it, your entire life will change. To make your ultimate vision happen, you need to grow and improve who you are - you need to become the type of person that can make your dreams a reality. It all begins with defining who that person is, who you ultimately want to be in this life.

Ask yourself these questions and get out your journal or spreadsheet to fill it in:

- **Who am I?**
- **Who do I ultimately want to be in this life?**
- **If I were to look up my name in the dictionary, what would it say?**
- **If there were no limits, who would I be?**
- **How would I define myself?**

Examples:

"I am an amazing son, brother, uncle, strategist, marketer, coach, speaker, etc..."

"I'm a mover and shaker of possibility."

"I'm physically fit, healthy, and vibrant."

Your Code Of Conduct

Your code of conduct are **the standards that you hold yourself to each day no matter what happens**. I usually make a list of about **10** standards that I strive to live up to, which is a good reminder for yourself to see how you're showing up in your life. This is something (along with the other sections of this book) that you can put up around your house to remind yourself of continually.

Ask yourself these questions and get out your journal or spreadsheet to fill it in:

- **What are the standards I want to hold myself to each day?**
- **What is my code of conduct?**

Examples:

"To be fun, playful, and outrageous."

"To be healthy and energetic."

"To be an example of all the good thats possible in peoples lives."

Your Categories Of Life For Continual Improvement

Now that you've discovered your ultimate vision, purpose, identity, and code of conduct, next is to get into the specific categories of your life. As we all know, there are categories for each areas of life that we continually need to improve and grow. If you don't grow, you die - it's as simple as that. The first step is to really identify the different areas of your life that are important you to continually focus on and expand.

I break life down into essentially **8 areas**, but it can vary for you depending on how many businesses you run or other areas that are important for you to focus on. Here they are:

1. Health & Fitness
2. Emotions
3. Relationships
4. Finances
5. Career/Business
6. Family
7. Friends
8. Spiritual

You could always chunk family/friends into relationships, or change it around - it's totally up to you. It's important to be flexible with this entire process and customize it to fit your life.

It's also important to make sure that you really make each category of your life compelling and exciting. The way that I do that is by changing up the language so that I can describe it in a way that sounds cooler. For example, instead of "Health & Fitness", I call it **"Physical Power: World Class Health And Fitness"**. Which would you rather focus on? The latter sounds far more awesome to me.

Ask yourself these questions and get out your journal or spreadsheet to fill it in:

- **What are the different areas of my life?**
- **Which areas of life do I need to focus on for continual improvement?**

Examples:

"Emotional Power: Unlimited Juice and Vitality"

"Absolute Financial Freedom"

"Internet Marketing Freedom Facilitator"

Your Ultimate Vision For Each Category Of Your Life

Once you've discovered the different categories of your life, next is to come up with an ultimate, compelling vision for each. You want to go through the same process as described above. Also, I really encourage you to be as specific as possible when describing your ultimate vision.

For your health and fitness, what would your vision really be? What would the weight be? What would your body fat % be? How would you look in the mirror? How would you feel on a continual basis? How would you feel when you wake up in the morning? You get the idea - but the more questions you can ask yourself, the more specific you can be, and the more likely you are to make it happen.

It's also a great idea to get pictures or images that you can put around your house, on your computer, phone, or anywhere that you can see it on a regular basis. This will help make it more real for you and really inspire you on a regular basis.

Ask yourself these questions and get out your journal or spreadsheet to fill it in:

- **What is the ultimate vision for each area of my health/fitness?**

- **What is the ultimate vision for my emotional life?**
- **What is the ultimate vision for my relationships?**

And so fourth, continue those questions for each area of life.

EXAMPLES:

"To be 170 lbs at 8% body fat, with unlimited energy and vibrancy throughout the day."

"To be financially free, making $1,000,000/year passive income from my internet businesses."

"To be in an incredible, loving, amazing, passionate relationship with the person of my dreams."

Your Ultimate Purpose For Each Category Of Your Life

Next you're discovering your reasons WHY and your ultimate purpose for each category of your life. Again, repeat the same process mentioned above. This is what will juice you and give you the motivation to really go after what you want.

Ask yourself these questions and get out your journal or spreadsheet to fill it in:

- **Why do I want to achieve this vision for my health/fitness?**
- **What will being financially free give me?**
- **How will having this amazing relationship enhance my life?**

And so fourth, continue asking yourself these types of questions for each area of your life.

Examples:

"To be able to look in the mirror and feel proud."

"To be able to travel the world and really enjoy my life fully."

"To never have to worry or stress about money again."

Your Identity For Each Category Of Your Life

Now it's time to discover your identity and who you want to be in each area of your life. By defining your identity and roles, you will be more motivated and compelled to spend time in these areas. Again, for you to achieve your ultimate vision, you need to enhance your identity and beliefs to be the type of person that can make this vision a reality.

If your identity for yourself is, "I'm over weight" or "I am lazy", then how are you going to make any vision a reality? **You need to change how you define yourself, which will therefor change your behaviours and how you will show up.**

Ask yourself these questions and get out your journal or spreadsheet to fill it in:

- **Who do I want to be in the area of health/fitness?**
- **What's a role or identity that will make me want to spend time in this area?**
- **How would I describe myself in the financial area of my life?**

And so fourth, continue asking yourself these types of questions for each area of your life.

Examples:

"I'm a lean, mean, fat-burning machine."

"I'm an agent of transformation."

"I'm a creator of the good life."

Your 1-Year/90-Day/30-Day Outcomes

Now that we've covered the higher purpose stuff, it's time to really focus on your specific goals and outcomes for each area of your life. For setting any goal or outcome, you want to make sure you're as specific as possible and each goal has a deadline. For example, you wouldn't want to have your goal be, "I want to lose weight." That's not clear at all - how much weight would that be? 1 lbs? 10 lbs? 50 lbs? **Clarity is power.**

I usually set 1-year outcomes, 90-day outcomes, then 30-day outcomes. Sometimes if your goals are too distant it becomes easy to disassociate from them. That's why having long-term and short-term goals are important. You also want to break down each goal. For example, if your 1-year outcome is to make $100,000 year, perhaps your 90-day outcome would be to make $80,000 a year, and then your 30-day outcome be to make $60,000 a year. Get it?

Ask yourself these questions and get out your journal or spreadsheet to fill it in:

- **What are my 1-year outcomes in each area of my life?**
- **What are my 90-day outcomes in each area of my life?**
- **What are my 30-day outcomes in each area of my life?**

Examples:

"I will make $100,000 a year passive income by December 31, 2013."

"I will be 180 lbs at 8% body fat and have unlimited energy by December 31, 2013."

"I will spend quality time with each member of my family at least once a week by December 31, 2013."

Your Action Plan

Once you've discovered your goals and outcomes, next you need to discover the specific actions you need to take to make them a reality. What would be the plan that, if you followed it, would guarantee that these goals become a reality? This is essentially the steps, the strategy, to reaching your destination. Again, you want to be specific with this. Don't just say, "I need to workout." Instead, your actions should be, "Workout 3x a week".

Ask yourself these questions and get out your journal or spreadsheet to fill it in:

- **What is my action plan for making these goals a reality?**
- **What steps would I have to take?**

Examples:

"Do research on which niche or market to get into."

"Run for 30-minutes, 3 times per week on the treadmill."

"Call each member of my family once a week."

Measuring Your Progress On A Weekly Basis

We're almost finished! First, I want to congratulate you for making it this far. If you actually went through this process and answered these questions for your life, **you have a specific plan for your life that 99.9% of the planet doesn't.** You're ahead of the game. It amazes me how many people have no idea what they want for their lives. But, you now do - you have a plan, a future, something to strive for. Congratulations, you have my respect.

Once you have clarity and all the information set up, the rest becomes easy. **The final step is to make sure that you have a regular ritual of checking in and measuring each area of your life.** For me, going through this process and reading my vision, purpose, goals, etc... every week works best. The more often you can measure something, the better - it will help remind you of what's really important in your life and why you're doing what you do.

As I said, the key piece is to make sure you're measuring yourself on a regular basis. As I said in the video, **progress is the goal (not perfection)** - it's what will make you very happy and fulfilled. And you must be growing and making progress in each area of your life, otherwise you're dying.

In my spreadsheet, I have a certain section where you can add the date for the week and then simply rate yourself on a scale from 0-10 in each area of your life. This is a good way to measure yourself by giving yourself a regular rating, so that you can see which areas are lacking and which ones are strong. If some areas are falling behind, all you need to do is put more focus into it for the following week.

Where focus goes, energy flows.

You can't manage something if you don't measure it. The more often you measure each area of your life, the better. For example, I always make sure I'm measuring my weight and body fat every week. The same goes with my finances and where my spending is going. Without measuring on a regular basis, how do you really know if you're progressing or not? You don't. That's why this has to become a MUST.

Putting This System In Action

We've come to the end of this book. It's crucial to make sure that you follow through and go through each of these steps - you deserve it for your life. It will give you the direction that most people lack. Not only that, but it will give you an edge over yourself and others. Think about how much better your life will be by having this system in place? How you will have more motivation, be more productive, and more fulfilled?

Once you have everything set up, it's imperative to make sure that you implement a weekly ritual to review things and make any modifications. Again, it goes back to the measuring piece. One of the biggest mistakes people make in society is they set their goals or outcomes for their life on New Years, and then they literally forget about it... the next time they check in is usually the year after, which is ridiculous. Don't fall into this mistake.

There was an interesting study done at Yale University where they surveyed their students about goal setting. Guess what they found out? **Only 3% of their students had set goals for their lives.** Isn't that crazy? But here's the crazier part - they followed up with the students 20 years later and discovered that the 3% that had set goals were much happier, more confident, and lived much more fulfilling lives. But that's subjective, right? Here's something more specific - **the 3% of students had a net worth that was worth more than the entire 97% of**

students combined. Isn't that staggering? THAT is the power of this - the power of having a life plan.

Give yourself this gift. It will change your life. If you have any questions, post them below by posting a comment. Or, if you'd like to share your vision or goals, I'd love to see them! Feel free to share. :-)

One last thing! If you want to learn more about this, I recommend Tony Robbins Time Of Your Life program, which goes into everything in much more detail.

Conclusion

Thank you for taking the time to read this Kindle book. I really hope that you received a lot of value from it. I know that I really enjoyed putting this together, as it's the best of the best of what Tony Robbins and many self-help experts out there teaches to manage your life, time and be productive.

If you take the time to really apply what you learned here and write down the answers to these questions, I can guarantee that it will transform your levels of time management and productivity. You will have a vision and purpose for your entire life, as well as each area. You will have clarity. You will be more productive and get more done.

The reason why I'm so passionate about this subject is because it has really changed MY LIFE. I attended a Tony Robbins event and programs and applied these very principles that he explains, and my productivity and motivation exploded. The stress went away, and I was more fulfilled.

So please, really make sure you apply this valuable information. If you don't commit to this, then chances are you never will. NOW is the time - don't leave it to later. As Tony Robbins says, make it a MUST!

And finally, I'd love it for you to go to where you purchased this book on Amazon/Kindle and leave a nice review of what you thought of the book. It's my goal to reach as many people as possible. As a "thank you" for writing a review, I will send you a FREE VIDEO and spreadsheet on how to further manage your life and put everything into action. It really is invaluable and will really influence your life.

All you have to do is e-mail me at stefan@projectlifemastery.com with a link to the Amazon/Kindle review that you posted, and I will reply back within 24 hours with the video.

Thanks, Stefan
http://www.ProjectLifeMastery.com

Printed in Great Britain
by Amazon